SECURING

— THE —

FUTURE

THE STORY AND STRATEGIES OF
OAKTRUSS GROUP

BENCHMARK BOOKS

Published by Freiling Agency, LLC.

P.O. Box 1264
Warrenton, VA 20188

www.FreilingAgency.com

PB ISBN: 978-1-963701-36-4
E-book ISBN: 978-1-963701-37-1

CONTENTS

PREFACE

As you read this book, you will notice that we refer to the company as Cyber Defense Labs for the majority of the narrative. This is intentional. During the course of our research, Cyber Defense Labs underwent a significant transformation, culminating in a rebranding as OakTruss Group. For clarity and continuity, we use the name Cyber Defense Labs until the later chapters, where we explore the reasons for and significance of this transition.

The change from Cyber Defense Labs to OakTruss Group represents far more than a simple name update—it is a declaration of the company's evolution in purpose, scope, and vision. This rebranding reflects a strategic shift from a focus solely on cybersecurity to a broader role as a partner in comprehensive business security and resilience.

OakTruss Group's new identity symbolizes a commitment to growth, innovation, and the flexibility required to meet the dynamic needs of its clients and the challenges of an ever-changing marketplace. This transition underscores the essence of the company's journey: one of reinvention, adaptability, and a relentless pursuit of excellence. We will share more about this near the end of this book.

INTRODUCTION

Benchmark Books is more than just a business series—it's a lens through which readers can understand the stories and strategies behind America's most exceptional companies. In a business environment where success demands innovation and meticulous execution, the concept of benchmarking has never been more critical. A benchmark represents a pivotal standard against which organizations measure their performance, offering a clear point of reference to evaluate financial health, operational efficiency, product quality, and strategic effectiveness. It's the navigational aid that helps companies identify strengths, address weaknesses, and stay competitive.

Our team of analysts and writers identifies the benchmarks set by industry leaders, providing a comprehensive look into the key factors driving their success. Each volume delves deeper than surface-level stories, offering an in-depth examination of the visionary leadership, innovative practices, and transformative strategies that have positioned these companies as industry frontrunners. Through meticulous analysis and insightful interviews with executives, vendors, and customers, Benchmark Books uncovers the core elements that make these organizations truly exceptional.

What Readers Can Expect to Gain

Readers of Benchmark Books gain more than an understanding of what makes top companies successful—they receive actionable insights that can be applied to their businesses and careers. Here's what you can expect:

- **Best Practices and Strategic Insights**
  Discover the frameworks and methodologies that have allowed these companies to set industry standards. Learn how to apply these strategies to improve your organizational performance.

- **In-Depth Industry Analysis**
  Each volume provides a comprehensive view of the competitive landscape, helping readers understand market dynamics and emerging trends to stay ahead in their respective fields.

- **Leadership Lessons**
  Explore the decision-making processes and leadership philosophies that have led to remarkable

achievements. Gain inspiration and guidance to cultivate your leadership approach.

- **Benchmarking Tools and Techniques**
  Understand how benchmarks are identified and applied, equipping you with the tools to measure your progress and achieve sustainable growth.

Benchmark Books isn't just about celebrating success—it's about providing a roadmap for those who aspire to achieve it. Whether you're a business leader seeking to refine your strategy, a professional aiming to sharpen your skills, or an entrepreneur looking to navigate the complexities of growth, Benchmark Books offers a wealth of knowledge to propel you forward. With its deep dive into the strategies of America's top companies, this groundbreaking series is an indispensable resource for anyone committed to excellence and continuous improvement.

1

BENCHMARKED: CYBER DEFENSE LABS

Cyber Defense Labs, located in Dallas, Texas, is passionate about helping companies better protect their business and build a culture of security. They specialize in simplifying the complexities of cybersecurity, empowering businesses to clearly understand their risks and take actionable steps to protect their assets.

In today's interconnected world, businesses face an unprecedented level of cyber threats, making robust cybersecurity protection not just a necessity, but a cornerstone of operational success. The consequences of inadequate protection are severe: according to IBM's 2023 Cost of a Data Breach Report, the average cost of a breach has soared to $4.45 million globally, with long-term reputational damage often compounding the financial impact. Moreover, cyberattacks are increasing in frequency and sophistication, with ransomware attacks alone rising by 13% year-over-year, as noted by Verizon's 2023 Data Breach Investigations Report.

Businesses that fail to implement effective cybersecurity measures risk exposing sensitive data, disrupting operations, and losing customer trust—consequences that can be catastrophic, especially for small to mid-sized enterprises. Investing in the best cybersecurity solutions ensures not only the safeguarding of critical assets but also strengthens customer confidence and long-term resilience, positioning companies to thrive in an increasingly volatile digital landscape.

This is where Cyber Defense Labs sets itself apart, offering comprehensive cybersecurity solutions tailored to address the complex and evolving threat landscape. By combining advanced technical expertise with a client-first approach, the company helps organizations identify vulnerabilities, implement proactive defenses, and build resilience against future attacks. This ensures businesses are not only protected but also empowered to navigate the digital world with confidence and clarity.

With services such as vCISO advisory, penetration testing, and vulnerability assessments, Cyber Defense Labs offers tailored solutions that align with each organization's unique needs. These offerings are designed to evaluate and enhance current cybersecurity programs, reducing risk and building resilience against evolving threats. By delivering clarity in an often-overwhelming digital landscape, Cyber Defense Labs enables organizations to focus on their core missions with confidence, knowing their cybersecurity strategies are robust and future-ready.

Cyber Defense Labs takes a comprehensive approach to strengthening an organization's cybersecurity posture, ensuring readiness to confront today's evolving threats. The process often begins with an in-depth analysis of the security environment, identifying gaps and uncovering vulnerabilities within the digital infrastructure. Leveraging tools such as penetration testing, vulnerability scanning, and cybersecurity assessments, the team delivers a detailed evaluation of potential risks. This foundational step provides organizations with a clear understanding of their risk landscape, serving as the basis for targeted improvements.

The next phase focuses on translating these insights into actionable preparation. With a thorough understanding of identified vulnerabilities, Cyber Defense Labs develops strategic plans to mitigate risks and enhance readiness. Services like tabletop exercises and incident response planning immerse teams in realistic scenarios, fostering the skills and confidence necessary to respond effectively to cyber threats. This proactive approach ensures that organizations are not only aware of their vulnerabilities but also equipped to address them with clarity and precision.

Once risks are identified and plans are formulated, the emphasis shifts to fortifying defenses. Cyber Defense Labs partners with organizations to implement tailored solutions that strengthen their cybersecurity framework. Through vCISO engagements, comprehensive risk management programs, and the refinement of policies and standards, the company ensures that defenses are robust, aligned with best practices, and capable of evolving alongside emerging threats. This critical step transforms strategic preparation into practical, sustainable action.

By following this structured methodology—analyzing vulnerabilities, preparing for incidents, and fortifying defenses—Cyber Defense Labs provides organizations with a resilient cybersecurity foundation. Each step is customized to address unique challenges, empowering companies to navigate the complexities of the digital landscape with confidence and clarity.

What makes Cyber Defense Labs truly stand out? This book dives into the answer. At its core is a team of accomplished leaders with a wealth of diverse, high-stakes experience. From former government intelligence and law enforcement professionals to seasoned CISOs with a proven track record of building resilient security frameworks, and executives who have steered billion-dollar enterprises through complex digital transformations, Cyber Defense Labs brings unparalleled expertise to the table. This distinctive blend of perspectives equips clients with both strategic guidance and actionable solutions, addressing immediate threats while embedding cybersecurity as a fundamental aspect of their organizational culture.

A Short History

Cyber Defense Labs was not always the innovative industry leader it is today. For years, the company struggled with an unfocused business model, fragmented services, and a lack of strategic clarity, leaving it vulnerable in a hyper-competitive and rapidly evolving cybersecurity market. Recognizing the urgent need for transformation, new leadership stepped in with a bold vision to realign the organization. Through deliberate strategy, disciplined execution, and a commitment to building trust, Cyber Defense Labs was reinvented into a specialized powerhouse in cybersecurity consulting, setting new standards for the industry.

To tell this turnaround story, we conducted extensive research and engaged deeply with the company's journey. Interviews with executives, staff, and clients illuminated the strategies, values, and decisions that shaped the company's evolution. Internal documents, performance reports, and case studies provided a foundation for understanding how Cyber Defense Labs transitioned from a struggling firm to a thriving industry leader. This book presents that narrative, offering insights into how the company overcame challenges, seized opportunities, and built a sustainable model for growth and excellence.

Lessons in Leadership

This book also offers practical insights for business leaders, entrepreneurs, and professionals in dynamic, high-growth sectors. It highlights actionable strategies for navigating organizational restructuring, fostering cultural change, and building resilience in competitive markets. Through a balanced blend of analysis and real-world examples, it provides a roadmap for leaders seeking to transform their organizations.

The story and strategies of Cyber Defense Labs offer readers actionable, practical insights for business leaders, C-suite executives, and professionals operating in dynamic, high-growth sectors, as well as start-ups. Key takeaways include:

- **How to Lead Through Change**
  Develop strategies to inspire teams, overcome resistance, and build a culture of adaptability during organizational restructuring.

- **The Power of Focus**
  Learn how narrowing your business's scope to its core competencies can drive exponential growth and market differentiation.

- **Building Financial Discipline**
  Understand the importance of aligning financial resources with strategic goals to create a foundation for sustainable success.

- **Navigating Competitive Markets**
  Explore techniques for thriving in fast-paced, high-risk industries where agility and expertise are critical.

- **Developing Resilient Leadership**
  Discover how to cultivate leadership qualities that enable you to lead in uncertainty and drive transformative results.

- **Strategic Decision-Making for Entrepreneurs**
  Gain insights into prioritizing opportunities, shedding distractions, and positioning your business for long-term success.

- **Lessons in Sustainable Growth**
  Learn how to balance innovation and operational excellence to scale your organization without compromising quality or focus.

The transformation of Cyber Defense Labs demonstrates that success in today's business environment requires more than technical proficiency. It demands a clear vision, disciplined execution, and a relentless focus on value creation. This book invites readers to examine these principles in action and consider how they can be applied within their organizational contexts.

2

THE STORY OF A TURNAROUND

Turning around a failing company is one of the most challenging feats in business, requiring a delicate balance of strategic vision, operational discipline, and cultural change. According to a study by Harvard Business Review, only 30% of corporate turnaround efforts succeed, with the majority failing due to resistance to change, misaligned priorities, or insufficient leadership. Leaders must often make difficult decisions, such as cutting unprofitable service lines, downsizing teams, or overhauling legacy systems, all while managing stakeholder expectations and maintaining employee morale. The process is further complicated by financial pressures—research from McKinsey shows that struggling companies typically have less than two years of liquidity, limiting the time to implement changes.

Cyber Defense Labs is the story of such a turnaround; it's not the same company it once was. It began as a modest cybersecurity firm offering a handful of services to small and mid-sized businesses. Over the years, the company struggled to keep pace with the rapidly evolving cybersecurity landscape. Although it had a loyal client base and a capable team, its growth had stagnated, and its service offerings lacked the focus and sophistication needed to compete in an increasingly crowded market. The company had the foundation for success but needed strategic leadership and a renewed sense of direction to realize its potential.

In 2018, a group of investors saw an opportunity to transform Cyber Defense Labs into a market leader. Recognizing the company's untapped potential, they acquired the firm with a clear mission: to reposition it as a premier provider of comprehensive cybersecurity solutions. One of their first moves was to bring in a new CEO, Bob Anderson, a seasoned leader with a unique combination of experience in law enforcement, crisis management, and private sector operations. Anderson's mandate was ambitious—revitalize the company's culture, refine its service offerings, and chart a path for sustainable growth in one of the most dynamic and competitive industries.

When Bob Anderson stepped into the offices of Cyber Defense Labs in January 2019, the scene could have been lifted straight from a cautionary tale about Silicon Valley startups. Anderson seemed an unlikely figure to steer the company out of its turmoil. His no-nonsense demeanor and sharp, analytical approach starkly contrasted with the disorganized, scrappy atmosphere that characterized the office. Yet it was precisely Anderson's outsider perspective—unburdened by conventional tech industry norms—that would ignite the dramatic transformation of this small, faltering company.

Cyber Defense Labs had long existed in a state of comfortable mediocrity. For years, its operations revolved around a "do-it-all" approach, taking on whatever projects were available to generate revenue. While this provided stability, it needed more focus to scale or thrive in a highly competitive market. Leadership immediately recognized the symptoms of a deeper problem: a business model stretched too thin, with service lines ranging from physical security installations to VoIP phone setups—all under the guise of a cybersecurity firm. The organization was a textbook example of a business stuck in the small-company trap, constrained by limited resources and lacking long-term strategic planning.

During the initial assessments, Anderson uncovered a series of inefficiencies and missed opportunities. The company needed more structure, financial oversight, and a coherent operational strategy. Employees, while skilled and dedicated, were overburdened by their roles. Hiring decisions had been reactive, made in response to immediate project demands rather than a thoughtful consideration of the skills needed for sustainable growth. This ad-hoc approach left the company out of balance, with some teams overstretched and others underutilized.

Anderson described the company's operations as more of a "high-tech yard sale" than a focused enterprise. Despite its branding as a cybersecurity firm, the business had no unifying mission or identity. This scattered focus was inefficient and damaged its credibility in an industry that prizes specialization and expertise. Clients were often confused by the company's broad but shallow offerings, which diluted its perceived value and made it difficult to compete with more focused competitors. The lack of a clear direction also hindered internal alignment, leaving employees uncertain about priorities and long-term goals.

The Challenge

The challenge ahead was clear: to transform Cyber Defense Labs from a struggling lifestyle business into a streamlined, growth-oriented organization capable of competing in a complex and rapidly evolving industry. This transformation required more than just cutting unprofitable services—it demanded a cultural and operational reset, and it would also take some time.

Anderson particularly emphasized the importance of patience and thoroughness during this critical transformation phase. "The first six months were all about understanding the business's disparate parts and how they fit together—or didn't," he explained. This detailed analysis served a dual purpose: it informed the leadership team's strategy. It helped build trust with employees, who were understandably apprehensive about the scope and pace of proposed changes. "We knew that being completely open with our people was crucial. We had to show them the numbers, explain our reasoning, and help them understand why these changes were not just necessary but vital for our survival and growth," he added.

Early conversations with employees and stakeholders revealed resistance to change and a willingness to acknowledge its need. Despite its inefficiencies, Long-time employees hesitated to abandon the familiar "jack-of-all-trades" model. Clients who had come to rely on the company's broad range of services expressed skepticism about a more focused approach. Internally, the board harbored concerns about alienating customers and reducing revenue streams, even as it became clear that the status quo was unsustainable.

Leadership approached these challenges with a blend of financial discipline and strategic vision. Anderson recognized that transformation would require operational restructuring and a shift in the company's culture. He focused on building trust, communicating the necessity of change, and demonstrating how a more specialized focus could unlock more significant potential for growth and success.

By methodically dismantling the tangled web of services and reshaping the company's identity, the company began to chart a path forward. Initial steps included eliminating unprofitable service lines, streamlining operations, and setting clear priorities for the business. This deliberate process was met with challenges, but it also began to reveal the underlying potential within the organization. Though initially skeptical, employees started to see the value of aligning their efforts with a focused mission.

Part of the transformation at Cyber Defense Labs involved a critical leadership realignment at the organization's top. Early in the process, it became clear that there were conflicting visions for the company's future, with key leaders divided on priorities and direction. This discord threatened to derail the company's ability to move forward. Through a process of intense and focused conversations, the leadership team confronted these differences head-on. Facilitated discussions clarified the organization's goals, helping to surface underlying concerns and establish a shared vision for the company's future. Out of this process emerged a newly aligned leadership team, unified in their commitment to the company's transformation and poised to drive progress with clear direction and purpose. This alignment at the top became a foundational element in ensuring the success of the company's broader restructuring efforts.

The transformation was not just about survival but about reimagining what Cyber Defense Labs could become. As the team moved forward, they understood that their success would hinge on their ability to instill discipline, foster collaboration, and maintain an unwavering commitment to the company's vision. This chapter marks the beginning of a journey defined by hard decisions and the promise of a brighter future for Cyber Defense Labs.

Today, Cyber Defense Labs is experiencing profitable double-digit growth and establishing itself as a formidable player in the cybersecurity industry. The transformation, guided by strategic leadership and a clear vision, has revitalized the company's operations and redefined its position in the market. The company now operates with a sharpened focus, a strengthened culture, and a robust suite of services that resonate with clients and address critical industry needs. Cyber Defense Labs continues to build on this momentum, leveraging its success to tackle new opportunities and set even higher benchmarks for the future.

Lessons for Leaders and Entrepreneurs

- **The Power of Focus:**
  Diversification without strategic alignment can dilute a company's mission and hinder growth. Leaders must identify and prioritize core competencies to build a strong, scalable foundation.

- **Cultural Reset is Key**
  Transforming a business goes beyond operational changes; it requires addressing the team's mindset and habits. Building trust and communicating a clear vision are essential for overcoming resistance to change.

- **Adapt Leadership Style to Fit the Context**
  Success as a leader depends on adaptability.

3

FINANCIAL STRATEGY AND GROWTH

For start-ups, developing and sustaining a solid financial strategy is often one of the most complex and challenging aspects of building a business. Research consistently shows that most start-ups fail within their first few years, with financial mismanagement cited as a leading cause. According to CB Insights, 38% of start-ups fail due to running out of cash or lack of funding, while others succumb to unsustainable growth models, poor resource allocation, or overextension. These pitfalls create a high-stakes environment where even minor missteps can snowball into insurmountable challenges. This is true for almost every start-up.

Cyber Defense Labs was no exception, grappling with the same financial pressures and structural weaknesses derailing countless others. In 2022, the company found itself at a financial crossroads. By this time Bob had interviewed 58 candidates for the position of Chief Financial Officer, and hired Marla Beckham, a seasoned C-suite veteran with both a financial and operations background.

She quickly recongized the company's precarious situation.

A significant client contract secured the previous year had brought substantial revenue, temporarily masking the organization's underlying structural issues. While the contract offered a much-needed financial boost, it also exposed critical gaps in the company's financial planning and operational strategies. The sudden cash flow triggered a wave of rapid hiring and investment, but these efforts lacked precise strategic alignment. Without a cohesive plan, the organization risked destabilizing itself as it scrambled to meet immediate demands. Compounding the challenge was the company's historical focus on short-term revenue generation, a reactive approach that left little room for sustainable growth practices.

"It was like watching a house of cards being built in a windstorm," Beckham remarked. "The money was there, but the planning wasn't. We were hiring left and right without considering the long-term implications." The lack of strategic foresight was particularly evident in how resources were allocated, and markets were targeted. Beckham's financial strategy and operational restructuring expertise became a vital force in tackling these challenges. The company soon embarked on a deliberate effort to shift Cyber Defense Labs from reactive growth to a sustainable, forward-thinking business model.

The Impact of the Client Contract

The 2021 client contract brought resources that enabled growth but revealed the company's lack of structured financial oversight. The influx of cash led to a hiring spree driven more by urgency than strategy. Teams expanded to meet immediate project demands without a broader view of the company's long-term needs. "It wasn't about building for the future; it was about firefighting," remarked Beckham. The pressure to scale quickly strained the organization, highlighting weaknesses in its operational infrastructure.

Anderson reflected on this period: "We were moving fast, but we weren't moving smart. The revenue boost was an opportunity but also showed us how ill-prepared we were to manage growth effectively." Positions were filled hastily, roles were poorly defined, and inefficiencies began to ripple through the organization. The absence of robust processes made tracking performance, accountability, or profitability challenging, further compounding the company's struggles.

This challenge is not unique to Cyber Defense Labs. Many start-ups need help managing the pressures of rapid growth, often leading to their downfall. Research by Startup Genome highlights that premature scaling is one of the top reasons start-ups fail, with 74% of start-ups collapsing due to scaling issues. The influx of resources or revenue often tempts companies to expand quickly without the necessary infrastructure, processes, or strategies. Another study by CB Insights found that nearly 30% of start-ups fail due to cash flow problems, which are frequently exacerbated by hasty, unplanned growth.

Without disciplined financial oversight and a clear operational roadmap, many start-ups burn through resources, unable to sustain their growth or pivot when market conditions change. Cyber Defense Labs faced a similar tipping point, but unlike many of its peers, it took the crucial steps needed to regain control and chart a sustainable path forward.

Diagnosing Financial Vulnerabilities

Upon joining the company, Beckham prioritized a deep dive into its financial health. Her analysis uncovered inefficiencies that the complexity of operations had obscured. Many service lines, though contributing revenue, could have been more affordable to deliver. The lack of standardized budgeting and financial controls compounded the issue, making it difficult to assess the true profitability of various offerings. She and the company's leadership team identified cybersecurity consulting as its core strength—a focus area where it could achieve higher margins and more substantial market differentiation.

"Core services became our north star," Beckham explained. "By realigning our resources toward areas where we could excel, we began to see a path toward sustainable profitability. The key was moving away from being everything to everyone and instead becoming exceptional at what we did best."

The financial review also underscored the reactive nature of past hiring and spending decisions, which had been driven by immediate needs rather than a cohesive strategy. This short-term mindset left the company with inconsistent staffing levels, unclear role definitions, and resource allocation that often prioritized urgency over efficiency. Recognizing these patterns, Beckham introduced a disciplined, structured approach prioritizing long-term sustainability over short-term fixes. She emphasized data-driven decision-making, leveraging analytics to assess profitability, operational performance, and resource utilization.

Aligning financial practices with the company's strategic objectives became a cornerstone of her plan. "We had to shift from thinking about survival to planning for sustainable growth," she explained. This approach also fostered a culture of accountability, ensuring that all departments understood how their financial decisions impacted the company's broader goals.

Restructuring for Sustainability

Armed with these insights, the company's leadership team undertook a comprehensive restructuring effort. This involved reassessing the company's service offerings and reallocating resources to align with its core consulting focus. Some of the most challenging decisions included shedding unprofitable service lines, such as the Managed Security Services Division (MSSP). While MSSP had been a significant revenue generator, its high costs and low margins dragged it on overall profitability. "There was a belief that MSSP was essential to our identity," Anderson said. "But when we looked at the numbers, it became clear that it was holding us back. We had to make the tough call to let it go so we could focus on what truly set us apart."

Convincing stakeholders to pivot away from longstanding service lines required persistent communication and transparency. Anderson, Beckham, and other leaders engaged employees, board members, and clients in candid discussions, presenting data to illustrate why these changes were necessary. "It wasn't just about showing the numbers," Beckham noted. "It was about helping people see the bigger picture. Change is hard, but it's easier when everyone understands the 'why.'"

Candid conversations with team members and stakeholders are essential during periods of organizational change, as they build trust, foster alignment, and reduce resistance. When leaders fail to communicate openly and transparently, uncertainty and confusion can take hold, often leading to disengagement and active resistance. Research from McKinsey & Company shows that 70% of change initiatives fail, with poor communication cited as one of the primary reasons. Without clear, honest discussions, employees may misinterpret the reasons behind decisions, fear for their roles, or feel disconnected from the company's goals.

In contrast, open communication helps create a shared understanding of the vision and the rationale behind changes, giving team members a sense of ownership in the process. For example, companies prioritizing transparent communication during restructuring efforts are 1.7 times more likely to achieve their transformation goals, according to a study by Harvard Business Review. Honest dialogue clarifies the "why" behind decisions and allows leaders to address concerns, answer questions, and mitigate fears, ultimately fostering a more unified and committed workforce. Neglecting this critical step can leave teams feeling undervalued and in the dark, which can derail even the best-laid plans.

Cyber Defense Labs demonstrated this power of open communication during its transformation by prioritizing transparency at every stage. Leadership engaged employees through regular meetings, detailed updates, and open-door policies, ensuring everyone understood the vision and rationale behind key decisions. This approach fostered trust, reduced resistance, and helped employees see their roles within the larger strategy, inspiring greater engagement and commitment. By addressing concerns openly and creating opportunities for dialogue, the company built a unified workforce that fully supported its ambitious changes, proving that honest communication is essential for successful organizational transformation.

Building a Financial Foundation

As the restructuring progressed, Cyber Defense Labs began to reap the benefits of a more disciplined approach to financial management. Resources were directed toward high-margin projects, and hiring practices became more strategic. Beckham and the finance team implemented robust financial controls and reporting systems, enabling the leadership team to track performance and make informed decisions. These systems brought clarity and accountability, creating a foundation for sustainable growth.

The company also fostered a culture of financial ownership within the organization. Employees were encouraged to understand how their roles contributed to the company's bottom line, creating a sense of shared accountability. "When people see the direct impact of their work on the company's success, they become more invested in the mission," she explained. Anderson echoed this sentiment, emphasizing that transparency was key to building trust. "People needed to see where we were going and how they fit into the bigger picture. Alignment comes when everyone understands not just what we're doing, but why we're doing it."

A profit-sharing program was also crafted and communicated to all team members, serving as a tool to enhance alignment and engagement during the company's restructuring. Profit-sharing programs are particularly effective for start-ups and growth-stage companies, as they provide a direct incentive for employees to contribute to the company's success while fostering a culture of shared ownership. Research from the National Bureau of Economic Research reveals that profit-sharing programs can boost productivity by 4-5%, as employees are more motivated when they see a tangible link between their efforts and financial rewards.

These programs are especially beneficial for start-ups in attracting and retaining top talent, as they offer a competitive edge over more prominent, more established companies. According to a study by WorldatWork, 68% of employees feel more engaged when participating in a profit-sharing program, and start-ups with such initiatives are more likely to see long-term loyalty from their workforce. By aligning individual contributions with company performance, profit-sharing incentivizes innovation and efficiency and creates a sense of belonging and purpose among employees.

This approach can be a game-changer for start-ups, and indeed, it helped foster a culture of cooperation and accountability for the company.

The Road Ahead

The financial restructuring at Cyber Defense Labs marked a pivotal milestone in its journey toward sustainable growth. Leadership's efforts to realign resources, streamline service offerings, and implement disciplined financial practices fundamentally transformed the company's operations and strategic outlook. However, this restructuring was not the endpoint but rather the beginning of a long-term evolution. The lessons learned during this critical period laid the foundation for a culture of efficiency and resilience in an increasingly competitive industry.

Looking ahead, company leadership is focused on positioning Cyber Defense Labs as a leader in the rapidly evolving cybersecurity landscape. Plans are in place to leverage the company's core strengths, foster a high-performing and innovative workforce, and maintain financial discipline to drive consistent growth. Leadership is also exploring strategic pivots, including investments in emerging technologies and targeted expansions into new markets, to ensure the company remains at the forefront of industry developments.

While the foundation for success has been set, Cyber Defense Labs recognizes that continued excellence requires ongoing focus, agility, and a commitment to staying ahead of the curve. The journey toward sustained industry leadership is still ongoing.

Key Takeaways

- **The Importance of Financial Discipline**
  Financial restructuring and disciplined resource allocation are crucial for turning short-term opportunities into sustainable growth. Companies must balance immediate needs with long-term planning to avoid instability.

- **Aligning Resources with Core Strengths**
  Focusing on core competencies and eliminating unprofitable or distracting service lines allows businesses to maximize efficiency and establish a strong competitive position in their industry.

- **Leveraging Profit-Sharing for Engagement**
  Introducing profit-sharing programs can align employee efforts with organizational goals, boost productivity, and foster a culture of shared

ownership, driving morale and performance during periods of transformation.

4

RESTRUCTURING FOR A SUSTAINABLE BUSINESS

Restructuring a business during rapid change involves fundamentally rethinking and reorganizing its operations, strategies, and structure to adapt to evolving market conditions and challenges. This process often includes redefining goals, reallocating resources, streamlining operations, and sometimes reducing or expanding the workforce to align with new priorities. According to a McKinsey study, only 30% of restructuring efforts succeed due to insufficient planning, poor communication, or a failure to address cultural resistance. In dynamic industries such as technology and cybersecurity, where market demands and threats evolve rapidly, restructuring often requires balancing short-term operational needs with long-term strategic objectives.

Restructuring Cyber Defense Labs was a unique challenge because it was not a start-up in the traditional sense; it had been operating for fourteen years and had an established client base and service portfolio. However, the company resembled a start-up in many ways, facing challenges commonly associated with early-stage businesses.

Its operations needed to have structure, financial planning was reactive, and its service offerings were scattered, leading to inefficiencies and a lack of strategic focus. The leadership team faced the complex task of transforming an organization that was already established yet fundamentally fragile. The challenge was maintaining the company's existing strengths while redefining its direction, operations, and culture to create a more resilient and scalable business. This required a start-up mindset—embracing adaptability and innovation—paired with the discipline and foresight of a mature organization to ensure the transformation was effective and sustainable.

In early 2023, Cyber Defense Labs faced the daunting challenge of reimagining its business to remain competitive in the rapidly evolving cybersecurity industry. Incremental changes would not suffice; the company needed a comprehensive overhaul to redefine its identity and focus. The leadership team initiated a sweeping transformation effort centered on aligning operations with core competencies, eliminating unprofitable service lines, and instilling financial discipline. This restructuring was not merely about cost-cutting but fundamentally reshaping the organization to ensure long-term sustainability and relevance.

Reassessing and Streamlining Services

A deep dive into the company's portfolio of services revealed a sprawling array of offerings that had accumulated over the years. Many of these services, while generating revenue, fell outside the company's core strengths and drained valuable resources. The Managed Security Services Division (MSSP) was a prime example. Despite its prominence and significant revenue, the division was plagued by high delivery costs, thin margins, and inefficiencies that made it unsustainable.

Financial analyses showed that while MSSP contributed millions in revenue, its costs consistently outpaced revenue. Research by Deloitte highlights a common pitfall in similar scenarios: companies often hold onto legacy services out of loyalty or fear of losing clients, even when those services hinder profitability. For Cyber Defense Labs, phasing out MSSP became a necessary step to focus on more lucrative consulting services where the company had a competitive edge.

The decision to discontinue MSSP met significant internal resistance. Employees who had invested years in building and maintaining the division were understandably reluctant to see it go. Stakeholders expressed concerns about losing long-standing clients who relied on these services. Leadership engaged in extensive dialogue, emphasizing that this move was not about erasing the past but building a stronger future. "We had to show that our focus was shifting toward delivering the highest value possible, even if that meant making hard decisions," Anderson explained.

Realigning Resources with Core Competencies

Research by Bain & Company shows that companies that focus on their core strengths outperform competitors by 36% over a ten-year period, underscoring the importance of specialization in building long-term client trust and loyalty. So once the decision to phase out unproductive services was made, leadership focused on reallocating resources to areas with higher margins and growth potential. This effort involved redefining roles and responsibilities across the organization, ensuring every team and department aligned with the company's new strategic goals. Again, financial discipline became a cornerstone of this process, with leadership implementing rigorous controls to track spending and prioritize investments that directly supported the company's mission.

This shift extended to client relationships as well. Clients accustomed to the company's previous "do-it-all" approach were informed of the transition and reassured that the new focus on core services would deliver more profound expertise and better outcomes. Leadership maintained open communication with clients, explaining how the changes would benefit them.

Indeed, open communication with clients is a cornerstone of successfully navigating organizational change, particularly when those changes impact the services or relationships clients have come to rely on. Transparent communication helps manage client expectations, reduce uncertainty, and build trust, essential for maintaining long-term partnerships. According to a study by PwC, 87% of executives agree that transparency is critical to sustaining client relationships during periods of transformation. For Cyber Defense Labs, keeping clients informed about the rationale behind strategic shifts, such as discontinuing certain service lines, was vital. Openly addressing how these changes would ultimately deliver greater value demonstrated the company's commitment to its clients' success. Moreover, engaging clients in dialogue about their evolving needs and expectations allowed the company to refine its focus and ensure its new direction aligned with market demands. Without this level of communication, companies risk alienating clients and damaging relationships, potentially jeopardizing their ability to sustain growth through the transition.

But these efforts were not without challenges. Some clients expressed concern about losing access to certain services, while others questioned whether the company could deliver on its promises within the more specialized framework. Anderson recounted, "Clients don't just need to know what's changing—they need to understand why. Once we explained how this focus would improve the quality of our work and allow us to deliver more value, the trust started to build. It was about showing them that we could serve them more effectively by doing fewer things better."

Over time, this approach began to pay off in meaningful ways. Clients appreciated the company's transparency and were impressed by the depth of its expertise in the newly defined areas. Many reported higher levels of satisfaction and trust, reinforcing the value of the strategic pivot. The company began to see increased engagement from existing clients and a growing number of referrals from satisfied customers who recognized the benefits of working with a more focused, specialized partner.

Managing Internal Resistance and Fostering Adaptability

As with any large-scale restructuring, the changes faced significant internal resistance. Long-standing employees and managers struggled to adapt to the new direction, and the uncertainty surrounding the transition created anxiety. Harvard Business Review emphasizes that transparent communication is critical during such periods, as it builds trust and reduces ambiguity. Leadership at Cyber Defense Labs embraced this principle, holding regular meetings, sharing financial data, and addressing concerns openly.

"Change management is about bringing people along on the journey," Anderson noted. "We didn't just dictate decisions; we invited collaboration and listened to feedback. When people feel included, they're more likely to support the process, even if they don't initially agree with every decision." This inclusive approach fostered a culture of adaptability and accountability within the organization. Employees were encouraged to take ownership of their roles in the company's transformation, helping to build a sense of shared responsibility for its success.

Building a Foundation for Growth

By the end of 2023, the initial results of the restructuring were evident. The company's focus on high-margin consulting services began attracting clients seeking deep expertise while eliminating unprofitable service lines freed up resources for strategic investments. Internally, the organization experienced a newfound clarity and sense of purpose. Employees embraced the shift toward specialization, recognizing the benefits of a more streamlined and sustainable approach. "We were no longer trying to be everything to everyone," noted Anderson. "Instead, we were focusing on being the best at what we do, and that focus was starting to pay off."

The restructuring also laid the groundwork for a broader cultural transformation. Employees were encouraged to embrace adaptability and innovation, essential qualities for navigating the fast-changing cybersecurity landscape. Leadership's balance of decisiveness and empathy set the tone for this new growth phase, fostering trust and collaboration throughout the organization.

Patience is critical during and after a restructuring process, as meaningful transformation takes time to materialize fully. Employees often expect immediate results or clarity, but leadership must set realistic expectations and consistently communicate that change is a gradual process requiring ongoing adjustments. A McKinsey study found that successful organizational change typically spans 12 to 24 months, underscoring the importance of maintaining a long-term perspective.

For Cyber Defense Labs, leadership emphasized to staff that while the restructuring was designed to create a more substantial and more sustainable company, the benefits would unfold incrementally. Regular updates on progress and acknowledgment of short-term challenges helped foster a sense of stability and trust. Encouraging patience also allowed employees to focus on adapting to their roles in the new structure rather than feeling undue pressure to achieve instant success. By reinforcing that transformation is a journey, not a sprint, the company created a more supportive environment where the entire team could remain aligned and motivated throughout the transition.

The Road Ahead

While the progress was encouraging, leadership remained acutely aware of the challenges ahead. Sustaining growth in the competitive cybersecurity industry requires ongoing vigilance, disciplined execution, and a commitment to continuous improvement. "Transformation is not a one-time event—it's an ongoing process," a company executive explained. We must keep asking tough questions, evaluating our performance, and refining our strategy to stay ahead."

With a solid foundation in place, Cyber Defense Labs is well-positioned to navigate future challenges and seize new opportunities. The lessons learned during this pivotal period guide the company's continued evolution, ensuring that it remains agile, resilient, and focused on delivering value to its clients and stakeholders. As the company moves forward, it remains committed to building a legacy of excellence and innovation in the cybersecurity industry.

Key Takeaways

- **The Importance of Focused Transformation**
  Even established companies can face challenges similar to start-ups, such as inefficiencies and a need for more strategic direction. Successful transformation requires aligning services, resources, and operations with core strengths to build a more sustainable business.

- **The Role of Transparent Communication**
  Open and ongoing dialogue with both clients and employees during restructuring fosters trust, reduces uncertainty, and ensures alignment with the company's vision, helping to smooth the transition and sustain relationships.

- **Patience and Long-Term Perspective**
  Organizational change is a gradual process that requires time, persistence, and clear communication. Setting realistic expectations and reinforcing a shared commitment to the company's goals helps teams remain engaged and resilient through the complexities of transformation.

5

CORE VALUES AND TEAM DYNAMICS

Many start-ups fail to define, establish, and communicate their core values, as they are often consumed by the immediate pressures of generating revenue and securing funding. According to research from Deloitte, only 23% of companies actively define and integrate their core values into everyday operations, and this percentage is even lower for start-ups, where the focus tends to be on rapid growth. This oversight can lead to fragmented cultures, misaligned teams, and more transparent decision-making processes, undermining long-term success.

Gallup data shows that organizations with well-defined values and strong cultures outperform their peers by 85% in sales growth and 25% in gross margin over ten years. By not establishing core values, start-ups risk creating environments where employees lack a shared sense of purpose, reducing engagement and productivity. In contrast, companies that prioritize core values early foster stronger team dynamics and build a foundation for sustainable growth and competitive advantage.

As Cyber Defense Labs redefined its operations and sharpened its strategic focus, leadership deliberately decided to prioritize core values as a foundation for success. While technical excellence was critical, they recognized that more would be needed to sustain the company in the highly complex and competitive cybersecurity landscape. Instead, fostering a team culture rooted in humility, transparency, and collaborative learning would be essential for achieving long-term resilience and exceptional client service.

This focus on core values was not an afterthought but a calculated strategy to align the organization's internal dynamics with its evolving mission. A strong, values-driven culture would help navigate the intricacies of cybersecurity and ensure that the company's employees were united in purpose and direction. Leadership understood that establishing these principles early would create a backbone for organizational stability, fostering trust and teamwork across all levels. By embedding these values into the company's operations, Cyber Defense Labs positioned itself to deliver technical solutions and a level of service and expertise reflecting its deeply ingrained commitment to excellence and collaboration.

Cultivating a Culture of Humility and Collaboration

A defining aspect of the transformation was leadership's emphasis on creating a team culture that valued humility and openness. Studies by Google's Project Aristotle highlight that psychological safety—where team members feel safe expressing ideas, admitting mistakes, and taking risks—is key to team effectiveness. Cyber Defense Labs sought to instill this principle across the organization. Team members were encouraged to embrace a growth mindset, recognizing that expertise was a journey rather than a fixed trait.

So Cyber Defense Labs built its culture on a team-first mentality, led by a leadership team emphasizing collaboration, ownership, and accessibility. Many leaders, having risen through the ranks themselves, brought a grounded perspective to employees' challenges, creating an environment where every team member felt empowered to contribute to the company's mission.

This ethos of humility and teamwork permeated the organization, breaking down hierarchical barriers and promoting unity. Cross-functional meetings, open-door policies, and shared accountability reinforced the idea that every employee had a stake in the company's goals. This culture proved instrumental during the company's transformation, enabling Cyber Defense Labs to build a resilient and adaptable workforce capable of tackling the complexities of the cybersecurity industry. The company fostered an environment where innovation and excellence could thrive by prioritizing trust, collaboration, and ownership.

Leadership also modeled these values, adopting an approachable and humble leadership style. Drawing from years of experience, they emphasized the importance of learning from both successes and failures. Leaders were accessible, promoting an environment where employees felt comfortable seeking guidance or sharing innovative ideas. This focus on humility created a foundation for collaboration, where employees across departments worked together to solve complex problems.

Hiring for Growth and Adaptability

For start-ups, hiring staff who possess flexibility and a start-up mindset is critical to building a resilient and high-performing team. Employees in start-ups often wear multiple hats, adapt quickly to changing priorities, and navigate ambiguity, making adaptability and problem-solving skills essential traits. Research from CB Insights reveals that 23% of start-up failures are due to team dynamics, underscoring the importance of hiring individuals who thrive in collaborative and fast-paced settings. These employees must excel in their roles and embrace a culture of learning, innovation, and teamwork to help the company scale and succeed in a competitive market. Start-ups that focus on hiring flexible, growth-oriented team members are better positioned to overcome challenges, seize opportunities, and maintain a strong, cohesive culture as they evolve.

So, as the company restructured, hiring practices were reimagined to align with the new culture. Rather than simply focusing on technical skills, the company prioritized candidates willing to grow, adapt, and contribute to a team-oriented environment. Research by LinkedIn found that 89% of recruiters say bad hires often lack soft skills, reinforcing Cyber Defense Labs' decision to emphasize adaptability and collaboration during recruitment.

During this phase, Cyber Defense Labs recognized the pivotal role of a quality interview process in shaping the organization's future. A well-designed interviewing process is not just about evaluating a candidate's technical skills—it's about ensuring they align with the company's values, culture, and long-term vision. By implementing structured interviews with scenario-based questions, the company assessed candidates' problem-solving abilities, openness to feedback, and adaptability to dynamic challenges. Research by the Society for Human Resource Management (SHRM) indicates that poor hiring decisions can cost businesses up to five times the position's annual salary, making thorough and thoughtful hiring practices essential. Cyber Defense Labs approached every hire as an opportunity to strengthen its culture, viewing each new team member as a critical piece of the organizational puzzle.

This commitment to quality interviewing helped build a team at Cyber Defense Labs that was technically competent and aligned with the company's collaborative and growth-oriented ethos, ensuring a strong foundation for sustainable success.

Leadership Rising Through the Ranks

A cornerstone of Cyber Defense Labs' culture was its leadership's dedication to fostering a team-first mentality. This approach was rooted in the experiences of many leaders who had risen through the ranks, gaining a grounded and relatable perspective on the challenges employees faced. By leveraging their journeys, these leaders cultivated an environment where collaboration and ownership were encouraged and expected. Employees at all levels felt empowered to take initiative and actively contribute to the company's mission, knowing their voices would be heard and valued.

This ethos of humility and teamwork had a ripple effect, breaking down hierarchical barriers and creating a culture of unity and purpose. Leaders across departments followed the CFO's example, adopting an accessible leadership style that bridged gaps between management and employees. Regular cross-functional meetings and open-door policies reinforced the idea that everyone had a stake in the company's success. The result was a workforce that felt connected and motivated, not just to perform their roles but to contribute to the organization's broader goals.

This team-first culture also proved invaluable as the company navigated its transformation. By fostering collaboration and encouraging employees to take ownership of their work, Cyber Defense Labs built a resilient and adaptable organization capable of meeting the dynamic challenges of the cybersecurity industry. Leadership's commitment to accessibility and humility created a foundation of trust, ensuring that every employee felt empowered to drive innovation and excellence.

Fostering Team Dynamics for a Dynamic Industry

The cybersecurity industry requires agility and adaptability, and Cyber Defense Labs recognized that its team had to reflect these qualities. Leadership implemented regular training and development programs to ensure employees could keep pace with evolving threats and technologies. However, the focus extended beyond technical skills, emphasizing the importance of communication, empathy, and teamwork.

Cross-functional collaboration became a cornerstone of the company's operations. Teams were structured to bring together diverse perspectives, ensuring that client challenges were addressed comprehensively. Regular knowledge-sharing sessions and team workshops enhanced cohesion, fostering an environment where employees learned from each other and shared their expertise.

While fostering a team environment is a common theme in company mission statements and leadership speeches, only some organizations successfully embed it into their daily operations.

Many companies pay lip service to collaboration and teamwork but need to create the structures, practices, and culture necessary to make them a reality.

Cyber Defense Labs stands out as an exception, actively prioritizing a team-first mentality in its operations. The company implemented cross-functional collaboration, regular knowledge-sharing sessions, and accessible leadership practices that broke down hierarchical barriers and encouraged open dialogue. Employees were empowered to take ownership of their roles while working cohesively toward shared goals. This intentional approach transformed teamwork from a "buzzword" into a foundational aspect of the organization's identity, demonstrating that true collaboration requires deliberate effort, continuous reinforcement, and an unwavering commitment to values that put people first.

The Impact on Client Relationships

The emphasis on team dynamics at Cyber Defense Labs profoundly impacted its client relationships, creating a noticeable shift in how the company delivered value. Employees who felt empowered and supported within the organization became more confident and proactive in client interactions. This cultural shift translated directly into exceptional service, as employees were equipped to go beyond the standard offerings and deliver innovative, tailored solutions that addressed clients' unique challenges. Clients began to take note, frequently praising the collaborative approach and the seamless integration of expertise across the company's teams.

The results of these efforts were striking. A client survey conducted six months after these changes revealed a 20% increase in satisfaction scores, underscoring the tangible benefits of fostering a strong internal culture. Repeat business also grew significantly, accounting for a larger revenue share as clients returned for additional services, reassured by the consistent quality and depth of expertise they experienced. Additionally, the company saw a sharp rise in referrals, as satisfied clients recommended Cyber Defense Labs to peers and partners. These metrics demonstrated the ripple effect of a well-aligned team culture, highlighting how an investment in internal dynamics can amplify external perceptions and drive sustained business success.

Sustaining the Culture

Leadership also adeptly recognized that maintaining this culture required continuous effort. Regular feedback loops were established to monitor team dynamics and address emerging challenges. One-on-one check-ins became standard practice, providing insights into team morale and areas for improvement. "When we invest in our people, we're investing in the company's success," Anderson explained. "Our culture isn't just about values—it's about creating a competitive advantage. A team that works well together delivers better results, period."

Indeed, sustaining a company's culture requires continuous effort and intentional practices to ensure that values remain embedded in daily operations. Research from Deloitte indicates that while 94% of executives and 88% of employees believe a strong organizational culture is essential to success, only 19% feel their company's culture is where it needs to be. This gap highlights how easily culture can stagnate or drift without consistent reinforcement. Maintaining a thriving culture involves regular communication, leadership modeling desired behaviors, and adapting to evolving workforce needs.

Sustaining Cyber Defense Labs' team-first mentality required ongoing initiatives such as feedback loops, employee development programs, and visible leadership commitment. These efforts reinforced the company's values and ensured that its culture could evolve to meet the demands of a dynamic industry.

The Road Ahead

As Cyber Defense Labs advanced in its growth trajectory, its leadership recognized that sustaining success in the dynamic cybersecurity landscape required more than technical expertise. The company's future would depend on its ability to maintain a cohesive team united by shared values of humility, collaboration, and adaptability. These principles, deeply embedded in the organization's culture, provided the foundation for navigating the complexities of an industry that demands both innovation and resilience.

The leadership's strategic investment in fostering core values and team dynamics positioned Cyber Defense Labs to face emerging challenges with confidence and cohesion. This focus on "how" the company operates, rather than solely on "what" it delivers, became a defining characteristic of its approach. By aligning culture with strategy, Cyber Defense Labs demonstrated that organizational success is built on the integration of purpose, people, and performance—a guiding philosophy that will continue to shape its evolution and competitive edge.

Key Takeaways

- **Define Core Values**
  Establishing and integrating clear core values early creates a foundation for strong team alignment and decision-making.

- **Prioritize Team Dynamics**
  Fostering collaboration, humility, and adaptability within teams strengthens internal operations and client relationships.

- **Commit to Sustaining Culture**
  Maintaining a thriving culture requires ongoing effort through leadership, employee feedback, and consistently reinforcing values.

6

RETHINKING INDUSTRY EXPERIENCE

When Bob Anderson, Marla Beckham, and other new leaders took the helm at Cyber Defense Labs, they brought with them impressive credentials: Anderson from law enforcement and crisis management, and Beckham from corporate finance and organizational transformations. Yet neither leader had technical experience in the cybersecurity industry—a point that raised questions about their ability to navigate the technical complexities and fast-evolving landscape of digital security.

Conventional wisdom often suggests that industry experience is a prerequisite for success, especially in fields as specialized as cybersecurity. However, data suggests otherwise. Research from the Center for Creative Leadership indicates that adaptability, learning agility, and people management skills are more significant predictors of leadership success than prior industry expertise. At Cyber Defense Labs, Anderson and Beckham demonstrated that while industry knowledge can be acquired, leadership qualities such as fostering collaboration, building trust, and selling a vision are indispensable.

The Value of Learning Agility

Cybersecurity is one of the fastest-evolving industries, with technologies, threats, and regulations changing constantly. For leaders stepping into this dynamic field without prior experience, the ability to learn quickly and adapt is critical. According to a Korn Ferry study, executives with high learning agility are five times more likely to succeed in roles requiring rapid adaptation.

Anderson and Beckham capitalized on their learning agility to immerse themselves in the technical and strategic nuances of cybersecurity. They engaged with subject matter experts, inside and outside of the company, industry conferences, and conducted detailed analyses of the company's operations and client needs. This hands-on approach not only helped them build foundational knowledge but also demonstrated to their teams that they were committed to understanding the challenges at hand.

Data supports the effectiveness of this approach. Leaders who actively engage in learning new skills and acquiring industry knowledge are 30% more likely to drive innovation within their organizations, according to research from Deloitte. By embracing a mindset of continuous learning, Anderson and Beckham positioned themselves to lead Cyber Defense Labs effectively, even without prior industry experience.

Building a Unified Team

One of the most pressing challenges at Cyber Defense Labs was the fragmented state of its workforce. Departments operated in silos, with limited interaction and a lack of coordinated effort toward shared goals. Communication across teams was inconsistent, and employees often found themselves unclear about how their roles contributed to the broader company mission. This disjointed approach stifled innovation, reduced efficiency, and created operational bottlenecks. Recognizing the urgent need to address this issue, Anderson and Beckham prioritized building a cohesive, high-performing team as a foundational step in the company's transformation.

Research by McKinsey underscores the importance of collaboration, showing that organizations with high levels of teamwork are 25% more productive and 30% more innovative than those with low levels of collaboration. Anderson and Beckham understood that fostering a culture of teamwork would not only boost morale but also enable the company to tackle the complex challenges of the cybersecurity landscape more effectively. To achieve this, leadership implemented several key initiatives: cross-functional teams to break down silos, regular town hall meetings to ensure alignment and transparency, and an open-door policy that encouraged direct communication between employees and leadership.

The results of these initiatives were transformative. Over time, Cyber Defense Labs began to function as a unified entity, with employees aligned around a shared vision and clear objectives. The shift was visible in both the day-to-day operations and long-term outcomes. Cross-functional collaboration enabled teams to share knowledge and resources, leading to more efficient problem-solving and innovative solutions. Regular town halls fostered a sense of inclusion, allowing employees to stay informed about the company's direction and feel invested in its success. The open-door policy, meanwhile, built trust and reinforced a culture of accountability and mutual respect.

This cultural shift not only improved internal operations but also had a significant impact on client outcomes. Teams were better equipped to collaborate on complex cybersecurity challenges, ensuring that clients received comprehensive, well-coordinated solutions. The alignment and synergy across departments translated into faster response times, higher-quality deliverables, and stronger relationships with clients. Ultimately, the transformation within the workforce became a cornerstone of Cyber Defense Labs' broader success, proving that fostering collaboration and unity can drive measurable improvements in both internal performance and external impact.

Earning Trust: Internal and External

Trust is a cornerstone of effective leadership, particularly in industries like cybersecurity, where clients entrust companies with their most sensitive information. Internally, Anderson and Beckham built trust by prioritizing transparency and accountability. They involved employees in decision-making processes, openly communicated about challenges and opportunities, and consistently followed through on their commitments.

Externally, the leadership team focused on developing strong relationships with clients, partners, and investors. According to PwC's 2023

Global CEO Survey, 82% of CEOs believe that trust is critical for long-term success, yet only 35% feel their organizations are viewed as trustworthy by stakeholders. Anderson and Beckham understood that building trust required more than delivering technical solutions—it demanded consistent communication, reliability, and a demonstrated commitment to client success.

These efforts to build trust had measurable outcomes. Client retention rates increased, and the company's reputation as a reliable cybersecurity partner grew stronger. Trust became a competitive advantage for Cyber Defense Labs, differentiating it in a crowded marketplace.

Selling a Vision, Not Just a Product

One of the most overlooked aspects of leadership is the ability to sell—not just products or services, but a vision. Effective leaders must be able to articulate a compelling future, aligning the organization's goals with broader trends and market needs. At Cyber Defense Labs, Anderson quickly recognized that to drive the company's transformation and foster growth, it was essential to clearly communicate the company's value proposition in a way that resonated with clients, employees, and stakeholders alike. This required a shift from a purely technical, product-centric sales approach to a more holistic and strategic message that connected with the broader business concerns of their target audience.

Research by Salesforce shows that 87% of executives believe storytelling is critical for building trust and driving engagement. Anderson and Beckham took this insight to heart, understanding that effective communication would be key to not only retaining existing clients but also attracting new ones. Rather than focusing solely on the technical aspects of cybersecurity, they reframed the conversation to position cybersecurity as a strategic enabler for business success. By emphasizing how robust cybersecurity frameworks could enhance trust, ensure resilience, and support business continuity, they tapped into the priorities of C-suite executives, who often saw cybersecurity as an increasingly critical component of their overall business strategy.

This strategic messaging approach proved highly effective in elevating Cyber Defense Labs' position in the market. The leadership team moved beyond the traditional perception of a cybersecurity company as a necessary but peripheral service provider. Clients began to view the company not just as a vendor, but as a trusted partner capable of addressing their most pressing cybersecurity challenges with a clear understanding of their broader business goals. This shift in perception strengthened relationships, deepened client trust, and set Cyber Defense Labs apart in an increasingly competitive landscape. By articulating the strategic value of cybersecurity, the company was able to connect with decision-makers on a much deeper level, paving the way for more meaningful, long-term partnerships.

Results That Speak for Themselves

The leadership team's efforts to adapt, build trust, and foster collaboration yielded remarkable results. Within two years, Cyber Defense Labs experienced exponential growth, with earnings climbing steadily and client satisfaction reaching new heights. These achievements were not the result of prior industry expertise but of universal leadership qualities applied with focus and discipline.

Data underscores the importance of these qualities. According to a Harvard Business Review study, companies led by adaptable and trust-focused executives outperform their peers by 25% in profitability and 30% in revenue growth. At

Cyber Defense Labs, these leadership principles proved more valuable than any specific technical knowledge.

Lessons for the Future

The transformation of Cyber Defense Labs demonstrates that industry experience, while valuable, is not always essential for effective leadership. What matters more is the ability to learn quickly, unite teams, build trust, and communicate a compelling vision. These qualities enable leaders to navigate even the most complex and fast-changing industries, turning challenges into opportunities for growth.

For organizations looking to thrive in uncertain times, the example of Cyber Defense Labs offers a powerful lesson: Success isn't about knowing everything from the start. It's about being willing to learn, adapt, and lead with purpose. As industries become increasingly interconnected and the pace of change accelerates, these qualities will only grow in importance.

Key Takeaways

- **Adaptability and Learning Agility Are Critical**
  Leadership success is less about prior industry expertise and more about the ability to learn quickly and adapt to new challenges. Leaders who embrace continuous learning and seek to understand their industry can drive innovation and effectively navigate complex environments.

- **Building Trust Drives Success**
  Both internal and external trust are vital for organizational growth. Transparent communication, consistent follow-through, and a commitment to shared goals foster team alignment, improve client relationships, and create a competitive advantage.

- **Leadership Transcends Technical Knowledge**
  Effective leadership is rooted in universal qualities like team building, strategic vision, and the ability to inspire confidence. These traits enable leaders to transform challenges into opportunities, even in industries where they lack prior experience.

7

TRANSPARENCY AND STAFF MOTIVATION

As Cyber Defense Labs embarked on its transformative journey, the leadership team recognized an essential truth: their most significant asset wasn't their cutting-edge technology or innovative solutions—it was their people. The structural changes and strategic pivots that defined the company's evolution would only succeed if supported by a workforce that was not only skilled but also deeply committed to adapting and growing alongside the company. For Bob Anderson and the team's leadership, building a resilient, skilled, and engaged team became a cornerstone of the organization's long-term strategy.

"Resilience isn't just about bouncing back," Anderson explained, drawing on his FBI and private sector experience. "It's about equipping people to face challenges head-on and emerge stronger. It's about building a team that doesn't just survive change—they thrive in it." This philosophy drove the company's approach to hiring, training, and fostering a culture that could meet the demands of a dynamic cybersecurity landscape.

Building the Right Team

Creating a resilient workforce required Cyber Defense Labs to balance attracting fresh talent with nurturing existing employees. The rapidly evolving cybersecurity field demands individuals who can think critically, solve complex problems, and collaborate effectively across disciplines. Recognizing this, Beckham spearheaded a targeted recruitment strategy beyond conventional hiring practices. She prioritized technical expertise in emerging areas of cyber and cloud security and candidates who demonstrated adaptability and a willingness to embrace change. "Technical skills can be taught," she emphasized. "What we need are people who are open to learning and growing—people who are prepared for the challenges of tomorrow."

Internally, the company implemented a comprehensive strategy to identify and develop talent. Employees who exhibited initiative and a commitment to learning were provided opportunities to lead projects, participate in specialized training, and transition into new roles. This approach not only addressed skill gaps but also fostered loyalty and a sense of ownership among employees. Clear career pathways further reinforced this commitment, enabling employees to envision their future within the company and actively pursue professional growth.

Training for the Future

To keep pace with the rapidly changing demands of cybersecurity, Cyber Defense Labs invested heavily in employee development.

This training extended beyond technical expertise. Anderson, drawing from his experience in crisis management, championed the development of critical soft skills. "Cybersecurity is as much about people as it is about technology," he remarked during a company-wide session. "We need teams that can communicate clearly, work under pressure, and make decisive decisions. These skills are essential for success." One of the most impactful initiatives was the mentorship program, which paired senior employees with newer hires. This dynamic learning environment fostered collaboration, preserved institutional knowledge, and strengthened relationships across the organization.

Fostering a Culture of Resilience

Resilience at Cyber Defense Labs extended beyond individual capabilities to the organizational level. Leadership prioritized transparency, ensuring employees understood the rationale behind significant decisions and were actively involved in discussions about the company's direction. Regular town halls, detailed updates, and open-door policies reinforced this commitment, creating an environment of trust and engagement.

The Impact of Collaboration

A critical component of the company's resilience was its emphasis on collaboration. Breaking down silos and promoting cross-functional teamwork became standard practice, enabling employees from diverse backgrounds to tackle complex problems with a shared purpose. This collaborative approach improved client outcomes and strengthened internal relationships, fostering a sense of unity and adaptability.

Anderson highlighted the connection between collaboration and resilience. "When teams work together effectively, they create solutions that are greater than the sum of their parts," he said. "Collaboration strengthens not just our results but also our people, making us better equipped to navigate future challenges."

Measuring the Results

The results of these initiatives were striking. Retention rates improved significantly as employees felt more invested in their personal growth and the company's success. Clients also noticed the difference, frequently commenting on the professionalism and adaptability of the teams they worked with. Cyber Defense Labs became known for its ability to retain talent in an industry plagued by turnover and burnout, a reputation that further strengthened its position in the market.

The Road Ahead

As Cyber Defense Labs looked ahead, the leadership team remained committed to fostering a resilient workforce. Anderson and Beckham understood that the challenges of the future would require not only technical innovation but also a team that could adapt and grow with the organization. With a solid foundation in place, Cyber Defense Labs was poised to navigate the complexities of the cybersecurity industry with confidence and purpose.

"Resilience isn't just about where we are today," Anderson said during a quarterly meeting.

"It's about where we're going and ensuring our team is ready for the journey. Every challenge we face makes us stronger, preparing us for whatever comes next. That's the true measure of our success." With this mindset, Cyber Defense Labs demonstrated that investing in people is not just good leadership—it's good business.

Key Takeaways

- **People are the Foundation of Success**
  Cyber Defense Labs recognized that its most valuable asset was its people, not just its technology or solutions. Building a skilled, engaged, and resilient workforce became central to its transformation, demonstrating that organizations thrive when they prioritize employee growth and well-being.

- **Investing in Training and Collaboration Yields Results**
  By implementing multi-faceted training programs, mentorship initiatives, and cross-functional teamwork, the company strengthened its internal culture. These efforts not only enhanced employee engagement and retention but also improved client outcomes, showcasing

the impact of fostering a collaborative and adaptable environment.

- **Resilience Requires Transparency and Well-Being**
  Leadership emphasized open communication and employee support through wellness programs and transparent decision-making. This approach cultivated trust, strengthened organizational resilience, and positioned the company to navigate future challenges with confidence and unity.

8

LEADING THROUGH CRISIS MANAGEMENT

Great companies are often defined not by their success during stable periods but by their ability to navigate crises effectively. Research by Deloitte reveals that 90% of businesses will face at least one significant crisis in a five-year period, yet only 17% are well-prepared to manage such events. Companies that excel in crisis management demonstrate agility, transparency, and strong leadership, turning challenges into opportunities for growth and trust-building. For example, organizations with well-developed crisis response plans recover 30% faster on average than those without. Beyond operational recovery, these companies often emerge stronger, solidifying stakeholder relationships, retaining customer loyalty, and reinforcing employee morale.

In cybersecurity, the stakes are even higher, as crises often involve breaches that threaten sensitive data, disrupt operations, and damage reputations. According to IBM, the cost of a data breach in 2023 averaged $4.45 million globally, highlighting the financial and operational toll of inadequate crisis management. Companies in this field must respond swiftly and decisively, as their ability to handle a breach can make or break client trust. Effective crisis management in cybersecurity is not just about technical expertise—it's about maintaining transparency, protecting stakeholders, and demonstrating reliability under pressure, making it a critical measure of success in the industry.

As Cyber Defense Labs scaled its operations, it encountered a unique set of challenges: balancing the intense demands of leadership while maintaining the resilience needed to guide its teams and deliver exceptional service. This dual focus—on operational excellence and relational trust—proved vital in navigating the complexities of its roles and the industry it served. It all came to a head during a crisis.

A Defining Crisis: Demonstrating Trust in Action

One of the company's most defining moments came during a high-profile cybersecurity breach affecting a key client. The breach was severe, with hackers infiltrating sensitive systems and leaving behind sophisticated malware designed to reappear even after initial remediation. Anderson received the call at 2 a.m. from the client's CEO, a level of accessibility he had promised to all clients. For Anderson, this was not an interruption but part of his commitment to the company's core value: trust.

Within an hour, Anderson had mobilized a cross-functional crisis team, swiftly transforming the company's headquarters into a fully operational emergency response hub. Drawing on his extensive law enforcement and crisis management background, he and his team ensured that every critical function—technical support, communication, and client liaison—was represented and equipped to act immediately. By 4 a.m., Anderson was leading a video call with the client's executive team, accompanied by the company's top technical experts, providing a clear and decisive action plan.

The atmosphere was tense, but Anderson's calm and focused demeanor set the tone for the team's response. "The stakes were immense," Anderson recalls. "This wasn't just about resolving a technical problem—it was about reaffirming our commitment to being there for our clients when it matters most. Moments like these define who we are—not just as a company but as a trusted partner." This swift, coordinated response underscored the company's ethos of reliability and partnership, demonstrating that trust is built in moments of challenge.

Coordinated Crisis Response

The company's response to the breach demonstrated a seamless alignment between leadership and technical expertise. Anderson led the charge, ensuring the team remained calm and focused despite the pressure. His crisis management skills, honed during his years in law enforcement, proved invaluable in breaking down the problem into actionable steps and keeping the team motivated. "Crisis leadership isn't about doing it all yourself—it's about equipping your team to succeed," he explains.

His transparency reassured the client that every decision was made with integrity and efficiency. "Clients need to see that we're not just solving the problem but also managing the process responsibly," he says.

The entire team rose to the occasion, and this coordinated effort extended into technical execution. Teams worked in shifts to eradicate the malware, restore compromised data, and implement robust safeguards to prevent future breaches. Real-time communication channels kept everyone informed, minimizing delays and ensuring every detail was noticed.

Lessons in Leadership Under Pressure

The breach underscored the strength of the leadership team's philosophy and approach, blending decisive action with strategic foresight and empathy. Their hands-on involvement reassured the client and the internal team, demonstrating that leadership during a crisis goes beyond technical expertise. It is equally about being present, remaining composed under pressure, and addressing immediate needs while focusing on long-term implications. The company's leaders ensured that every decision was intentional, balancing swift action with a thoughtful strategy to minimize disruptions and rebuild confidence.

The client's feedback following the crisis highlighted the profound impact of this approach. Not only were the compromised systems restored efficiently, but the client's trust in the company deepened significantly. The client's CEO remarked, "You didn't just fix our problem—you stood by us every step of the way. That's a rare quality in this industry." This outcome reinforced the idea that in moments of crisis, authentic leadership isn't just about resolving technical challenges but about demonstrating unwavering support and commitment to building enduring relationships.

Transforming Crisis into Opportunity

The aftermath of the breach became a pivotal moment for Cyber Defense Labs, marking a turning point in how the company approached both crisis management and organizational culture. The leadership team facilitated a comprehensive debrief, where team members were encouraged to share their experiences, insights, and suggestions for improvement. This open and inclusive process not only acknowledged the efforts of employees but also highlighted areas for refinement. The resulting feedback loop led to tangible advancements, including implementing a tiered incident response system that allowed for a more precise allocation of resources based on threat levels and a centralized communication platform designed to ensure real-time updates across departments during future crises.

Beyond operational improvements, the experience sparked a cultural transformation within the organization. Employees who participated in the response witnessed how the company's core values—partnership, expertise, and trust—were implemented under extreme pressure. This alignment between stated values and real-world operations fostered a more profound sense of pride and commitment among team members. It also strengthened employee engagement, as individuals felt their contributions were recognized and meaningful. The event reinforced a shared sense of purpose, demonstrating that every role within the company played a vital part in its success. This cultural shift became a foundation for greater unity and adaptability, ensuring the organization was better prepared for future challenges and more cohesive and motivated to meet them head-on.

Balancing Leadership Demands with Well-Being

Leading through crises requires technical and strategic expertise and personal resilience. The leadership team at Cyber Defense Labs understood that to effectively guide their organization, they needed to manage the intense demands of their roles while maintaining their well-being. This challenge is not unique to them; research by McKinsey shows that 80% of executives experience burnout, with the relentless pace of high-stakes decision-making being a primary contributor. Studies by the American Psychological Association further highlight that leaders who neglect self-care are likelier to make reactive, short-sighted decisions, ultimately impacting organizational outcomes.

Anderson and the leadership team at Cyber Defense Labs adopted proactive strategies to ensure they could sustain their performance without compromising their health. One key approach was creating intentional time for reflection and recovery. "You can't pour from an empty cup," Anderson emphasized. "Leadership is about showing up for your team, which means taking care of yourself first." They scheduled regular breaks during demanding periods, using this time to assess broader perspectives and recalibrate their focus.

Leaders prioritized physical and mental health in high-pressure moments through activities like exercise, mindfulness practices, and setting boundaries around non-critical tasks. This emphasis on balance extended to their decision-making processes. "It's not just about reacting in the moment," one noted. "It's about ensuring your decisions are grounded and strategic, which only happens when you're operating at your best," remarked Beckham.

This commitment to well-being also served as a model for the broader organization, fostering a culture that encouraged employees to prioritize their health and resilience. By demonstrating that well-being was essential even during crises, the leadership team reinforced a vital message: sustainable success depends on what you accomplish and how you sustain the energy and focus to achieve it.

The Road Ahead

Cyber Defense Labs emerged from the crisis more assertive, not just in its technical capabilities but in its culture and leadership. Anderson and Beckham's ability to balance the demands of their roles with the needs of their clients and employees became a defining characteristic of the company. They built a foundation for long-term resilience through trust, transparency, and a commitment to continuous improvement.

For Anderson, the experience reinforced a core belief: "Leadership isn't about avoiding challenges—it's about facing them head-on and turning them into opportunities for growth." Beckham echoed this sentiment, adding, "Every crisis is a chance to show who you are as a company. When you put your values into action, you don't just solve problems—you build lasting trust."

As Cyber Defense Labs looks to the future, the lessons from this chapter remain central to its identity. In an industry where the stakes are high and trust is paramount, the company's leadership and crisis management approach stands as a testament to the power of resilience, collaboration, and unwavering commitment.

Key Takeaways

- **Leadership During a Crisis Is About Balance**
  Effective crisis leadership requires balancing swift, decisive actions with empathy and strategic foresight, ensuring immediate needs and long-term impacts are addressed.

- **Crisis Moments Build Trust and Define Partnerships**
  How an organization responds during challenges can strengthen client relationships and reinforce trust, turning potential setbacks into opportunities for lasting partnerships.

- **Resilience Comes from Preparation and Culture**
  A strong internal culture and proactive crisis protocols equip organizations to handle crises effectively, ensuring teams are aligned and empowered to navigate complex challenges confidently.

9

OWNING THE MISSTEPS

Great leadership is not about avoiding mistakes—it's about owning them. In high-pressure environments, particularly in industries as complex and fast-paced as cybersecurity, missteps are inevitable. What distinguishes effective leaders is their ability to acknowledge errors, analyze what went wrong, and pivot decisively toward a better path. This combination of humility, transparency, and strategic recalibration fosters trust among team members and stakeholders, turning setbacks into valuable learning opportunities.

For Cyber Defense Labs, this philosophy was put to the test during a period of aggressive expansion that revealed critical flaws in the company's approach to sales. This chapter delves into a pivotal moment in the organization's journey—a costly and nearly catastrophic misstep that, if left unaddressed, could have derailed its trajectory. However, the leadership team's willingness to confront the issue head-on, reexamine its strategy, and make bold changes ultimately set the stage for a transformative turnaround.

The High Cost of Relentless Expansion

In the years following its acquisition, Cyber Defense Labs embarked on an ambitious growth strategy driven by an urgent desire to capture market share and solidify its position in the cybersecurity industry. Under this directive, the company aggressively expanded its sales team, bringing on waves of new hires and setting increasingly ambitious revenue targets. Millions of dollars were funneled into these initiatives, and the pressure on the sales team was immense.

The leadership's approach was straightforward: more salespeople, higher quotas, and relentless effort would translate into greater revenue. At face value, this strategy seemed logical. After all, a larger sales force should, theoretically, result in more deals closed. But as the months turned into years, the anticipated results failed to materialize. Revenue stagnated, and the company struggled to achieve a meaningful return on its substantial investment.

Doubling Down Without Results

Despite the lack of progress, management initially resisted reevaluating its strategy. Convinced that the solution lay in pushing harder, sales leadership doubled down on its efforts, further expanding the sales team and intensifying quotas. Millions more were allocated to sales initiatives, and expectations soared. However, this approach only deepened the company's challenges.

The relentless drive to deliver results began to take a toll. The sales team was stretched thin, morale faltered, and frustration mounted as the gap between effort and outcomes widened. The leadership team was confused and increasingly desperate, unable to understand why their aggressive strategy wasn't producing the desired results. Their reluctance to pivot created a cycle of inefficiency, consuming valuable resources while yielding little in return.

Identifying the Core Issues

Eventually, leadership recognized the need for a course correction. A comprehensive analysis of the sales strategy revealed three critical issues undermining the company's performance:

A Transactional Approach to Sales

The sales team was focused on selling individual products and services—"widgets"—rather than cultivating long-term, value-driven relationships with clients. This transactional mindset limited repeat business and failed to align with the company's broader goal of becoming a trusted cybersecurity partner. Research from Gartner underscores the importance of a relationship-focused approach, showing that companies prioritizing strategic partnerships experience a 47% higher customer retention rate and a 20% increase in revenue over five years. Cyber Defense Labs' reliance on one-off sales was not only unsustainable but also stifling its ability to build lasting client relationships.

Saying "Yes" Too Often

The team had developed a habit of accepting deals indiscriminately, prioritizing volume over profitability. While this approach created the illusion of momentum, it came at a significant cost. Contracts were often taken on with slim or negative margins, straining the company's resources without contributing meaningfully to its bottom line. According to McKinsey, businesses that focus on quality over quantity in their client portfolios see a 25% increase in profit margins. By failing to prioritize strategic, high-value opportunities, Cyber Defense Labs was wasting resources and missing the chance to build a more sustainable, profitable client base.

Targeting the Wrong Audience

The sales team was primarily targeting IT middle-management—individuals who, while influential, lacked the decision-making authority and budgetary control needed to secure high-value partnerships. This misalignment meant that even when deals were closed, they were often smaller and less strategic than the company needed to achieve its growth objectives. The leadership team realized that to drive meaningful change, they needed to shift their focus to top-level decision-makers, such as CEOs and CFOs, who had the power to invest in comprehensive cybersecurity solutions.

A Bold Pivot: Shifting the Focus

Armed with these insights, the leadership team made the bold decision to scrap the existing sales strategy and start fresh. This was no small undertaking. It required not only a reorganization of the sales team but also a fundamental shift in the company's approach to business development.

Bob Anderson took the lead, hitting the road to engage directly with CEOs and other top executives. His goal was to bypass gatekeepers and build relationships with the individuals who had the authority, budget, and strategic vision to recognize the value Cyber Defense Labs could bring to their organizations.

Anderson's pitch was tailored for the boardroom, not the server room. Instead of focusing on technical details, he framed cybersecurity as a business enabler, emphasizing its role in protecting trust, brand reputation, and operational resilience. "Cybersecurity isn't just a technical problem; it's a boardroom priority," he would explain. This approach resonated with CEOs, who began to see Cyber Defense Labs not just as a vendor but as a strategic partner capable of addressing their most pressing challenges.

Reaping the Rewards of Change

The shift in strategy paid off in dramatic fashion. Within months, the company began to see tangible results. Deals closed faster, contract values increased, and the company's reputation among high-level executives grew stronger. CEOs who had initially been skeptical became advocates, referring Cyber Defense Labs to their peers and inviting the company into strategic conversations about enterprise risk management and digital transformation.

"The numbers soon looked so good, they looked fake!" Anderson remarked, reflecting on the exponential growth that followed the strategic reset. By focusing on trust, strategic partnerships, and profitability, the company turned its fortunes around and positioned itself as a leader in the cybersecurity industry.

Lessons in Leadership

This chapter underscores a fundamental truth about leadership: the willingness to acknowledge mistakes and pivot is essential for long-term success. Research by the Harvard Business Review shows that leaders who admit to errors and take accountability are 50% more likely to retain employee trust and engagement during challenging times. By embracing this philosophy, Cyber Defense Labs not only overcame a critical misstep but also laid the groundwork for a more focused, resilient, and sustainable future.

Mistakes are inevitable, but the ability to learn from them and adapt is what separates great leaders from the rest. For Cyber Defense Labs, this journey of self-reflection and reinvention transformed a near-catastrophe into a defining moment of growth and success. It's a lesson that extends far beyond cybersecurity, offering valuable insights for any organization navigating the complexities of a competitive marketplace.

Key Takeaways

- **Leadership Requires Accountability**
  Effective leadership means acknowledging mistakes, learning from them, and taking corrective action. Mistakes are inevitable, but addressing them openly builds trust, fosters transparency, and sets the stage for meaningful improvement.

- **Strategic Realignment Is Essential**
  When strategies fail to deliver results, doubling down without reassessment can waste valuable resources. Leaders must step back, conduct rigorous analysis, and recalibrate their approach to align efforts with the organization's goals.

- **Focusing on the Right Audience Matters**
  Targeting the correct decision-makers and framing the message around their strategic priorities is key to driving sustainable growth. Building relationships with executives, rather than relying on transactional sales, can transform a struggling strategy into a winning one.

10

LOOKING AHEAD— THE EVOLUTION TO OAKTRUSS GROUP

In business leadership, there is no finish line. This simple yet profound truth resonates deeply as Cyber Defense Labs embarks on the next phase of its journey, transforming into OakTruss Group. This evolution signifies more than just a name change; it marks the company's commitment to broadening its mission, expanding from a focus solely on cybersecurity to becoming a comprehensive business consultancy specializing in areas critical to organizational security.

This transition underscores an important reality: leading a business or organization is not about arriving at a single point of success but about continuously adapting, evolving, and growing to meet the demands of an ever-changing landscape. Just as a company can never rest on its laurels, leadership is an ongoing process of learning, innovating, and pushing boundaries.

A Name that Reflects Purpose

The name "OakTruss Group" was chosen intentionally, reflecting strength, stability, and interconnectedness. The oak symbolizes resilience and longevity, while the truss represents structural integrity and support—elements that are central to the company's new mission. The rebrand is not just cosmetic; it signals a strategic shift in focus, aimed at helping businesses navigate a broader range of risks beyond cybersecurity, including operational, financial, and reputational challenges.

This expanded mission aligns with data from Deloitte, which shows that 79% of executives believe that addressing non-technical risks, such as regulatory compliance and organizational culture, is as critical to business success as managing technical threats. OakTruss Group aims to be at the forefront of this integrated approach to business security, providing clients with a holistic perspective on risk and resilience.

No Finish Line: Leadership in Perpetual Motion

The idea that "there is no finish line" is a guiding principle for OakTruss Group's leadership team. For Bob Anderson and the broader leadership, this philosophy reflects their understanding that success is not a destination but a journey. Organizations that fail to embrace this mindset risk stagnation and irrelevance in industries that demand constant innovation.

Consider this: research by McKinsey & Company shows that companies that regularly reinvent themselves are twice as likely to outperform their peers in terms of revenue growth and profitability. Yet, only 10% of businesses successfully make such transformations. The transition from Cyber Defense Labs to OakTruss Group represents a deliberate effort to remain ahead of the curve, embracing change not as a challenge but as an opportunity to redefine the company's role in a dynamic marketplace.

This mindset also instills a culture of continuous improvement within OakTruss Group. By viewing each milestone as a stepping stone rather than a finish line, the leadership encourages its team to remain adaptable, curious, and forward-thinking. This approach ensures that the organization is not only prepared to address today's challenges but also poised to anticipate and navigate the uncertainties of tomorrow. It is this commitment to perpetual growth and reinvention that will define OakTruss

Group's legacy and position it as a leader in an ever-evolving business landscape.

As Cyber Defense Labs evolved into OakTruss Group, the company's leadership structure adapted to meet the demands of its expanding vision. Bob Anderson transitioned to Managing Partner, focusing on strategic growth, high-level partnerships, and long-term planning. At the same time, Marla Beckham assumed the position of President, taking charge of day-to-day operations and driving execution across the organization. This realignment of roles reflected the leadership team's commitment to ensuring the company's structure supported its evolving goals. Research by Deloitte highlights that redefining leadership roles is critical to maintaining operational efficiency and strategic focus as companies grow. By leveraging Anderson's visionary leadership and Beckham's operational expertise, the company ensured a balanced approach to its dual objectives of innovation and execution. This strategic shift not only positioned OakTruss Group for sustained growth but also demonstrated the importance of aligning leadership roles with the company's stage of development and future ambitions.

Expanding Beyond Cybersecurity

While cybersecurity will remain a core compe-tency, OakTruss Group's vision extends far beyond technical defenses. The company will leverage its expertise in risk management and stra-tegic planning to help businesses tackle broader challenges, such as insider risk, regulatory compli-ance, crisis management, operational resilience, and even leadership development. This expansion reflects a growing demand for integrated business consulting, as companies increasingly recognize the interconnected nature of modern risks.

A recent PwC study revealed that 60% of CEOs believe their organizations face more complex risks today than they did three years ago. This complexity requires a multidisciplinary approach—one that combines technical expertise with strategic insight. OakTruss Group aims to fill this gap, offering clients a one-stop solution for navigating uncer-tainty and building sustainable success.

Building a Legacy of Trust and Value

The evolution to OakTruss Group is also about creating a legacy that extends beyond individual transactions or short-term gains. The leadership team envisions a company that not only protects businesses but also empowers them to thrive. This means fostering long-term relationships based on trust, delivering value that goes beyond the immediate scope of services, and contributing to the broader business community.

Trust remains a cornerstone of this mission. Research by Edelman shows that 67% of executives consider trust their most valuable intangible asset. By maintaining its commitment to transparency, collaboration, and excellence, OakTruss Group seeks to deepen its reputation as a trusted partner for businesses navigating complex challenges.

A Culture of Continuous Improvement

Internally, the transition to OakTruss Group represents an opportunity to reinforce the company's culture of resilience, innovation, and continuous improvement. Employees will be encouraged to develop new skills, embrace interdisciplinary approaches, and think creatively about solving complex problems. The company's investment in professional development and cross-functional collaboration will ensure that the team remains agile and prepared for future challenges.

A study by Gartner found that organizations with high levels of employee engagement are 21% more profitable than their peers. By prioritizing its people and fostering a culture of growth, OakTruss Group aims to harness the full potential of its workforce, driving innovation and delivering exceptional results for clients.

The Road Ahead

Looking to the future, OakTruss Group recognizes that the journey will be filled with new challenges and opportunities. The company's evolution will require not only strategic foresight but also the courage to embrace uncertainty and the humility to learn from setbacks. However, with a clear vision, strong leadership, and a dedicated team, OakTruss Group is well-positioned to navigate the complexities of the modern business landscape.

"There is no finish line" is not just a philosophy for OakTruss Group—it's a call to action. It's a reminder that success requires relentless effort, a commitment to excellence, and the ability to adapt to the unknown. As the company takes its next steps, it remains focused on its mission to help businesses build not just security but resilience, not just systems but trust, and not just solutions but lasting value.

In embracing this new chapter, OakTruss Group reaffirms its dedication to leadership, innovation, and partnership. The path forward is uncharted, but one thing is certain: the journey is far from over, and the best is yet to come.